This book is dedicated to all the staff, volunteers and supporters who have helped Duchess of Kent House since its opening in 1992 providing invaluable specialist palliative care to thousands of patients from Berkshire and surrounding districts.

help your local
H O S P I C E

Blooming Famous
a gardening compendium from the famous and not-so-famous
including some Delicious Famous recipes

Published by
Duchess of Kent House Trust
22 Liebenrood Road
READING RG30 2DX

Telephone: 0118 939 4889
Fax: 0118 951 2692
E-mail: info@duchessofkenthouse.org.uk
Website: www.duchessofkenthouse.org.uk

Further copies of this and other publications are available from Duchess of Kent House Trust at the above address.

Duchess of Kent House Trust is a Registered Charity no.1085912
A Company Limited by Guarantee: registered in England no. 4032552
Copyright © Duchess of Kent House Trust, 2005
The moral right of the copyright-holder is asserted in accordance with the Copyrights, Design and Patents Act 1988.

All rights reserved. No part of this book may be stored in a retrieval system or reproduced in any form without prior written permission from the publisher. This book is sold subject to the condition that it must not be lent, re-sold or otherwise circulated without the publisher's prior written permission in any form of binding or cover other than that in which it is published, and without a similar condition being imposed on the subsequent purchaser.

ISBN: 0-9543661-2-3   Bar code:
First Edition 2005.
Editor: George Solly
Designer: Ralph Solly
Illustrations: see acknowledgements

978 09 54 366124

Foreword

The gardens at Duchess of Kent House were designed by Robin Lane Fox in the early nineties to accommodate the needs of the patients and their visitors, with consideration for ease of maintenance. Tucked away at the back of the Dellwood site first impressions when coming to Duchess of Kent House are of raised brick flower beds and car park. However behind the buildings to the east and south are the 'hidden' gardens the patients so appreciate.

Taken from the original brochure

Architecturally, each of the single and four bedded wards has French windows looking out onto a paved area where patients and their visitors can sit with some degree of seclusion. The eastern side of the site is parallel to Parkside Road, which at the time of writing is undergoing extensive redevelopment with old commodious Victorian and Edwardian buildings being knocked down in favour of higher density flats and houses in the modern style. Although there is about 20 metres to the boundary wall our quiet haven is under threat from noise pollution so it has been decided to heighten the existing brick wall and introduce some screen planting. Beyond each patio are herbaceous borders well stocked with plants of all descriptions and a path running close to the rear boundary.

In 2002, in celebration of our 10th anniversary, Rose's Garden Room was built onto the in-patients' reception / sitting area, with doors inviting the garden into the House and vice versa. Over the years donations and bequests have provided much garden furniture, the conservatory, the hanging basket irrigation system, water features, a children's playhouse, a wishing well, a greenhouse, many stock plants and much more besides, in addition to Rose's Garden Room.

To the south the garden changes being more of a courtyard with raised beds nestling between the arms of the 'U' shape of that part of the building which houses more wards, the Sanctuary, The Green (day therapy), admin and treatment rooms. The wards still have their patios but are more open.

Contractors do the grass cutting but it is the band of gardening volunteers who really work hard to look after the detail of the gardens. Using the greenhouse and their own gardens they plant seeds, propagate and transplant providing the gardens with their variety. Any excess plant stock is sold off with donations going back to the charity. The year 2004 was the first to have a Garden Open Day here so that friends and relatives of patients plus our supporters could appreciate our gardens in their entirety.

The south garden is the home to the annual Light Up A Life carol service held on the first Friday in December. Four hundred members of the public crowd in to celebrate the lives of loved ones (not necessarily treated here) with candles and other lights. Local dignitaries and choirs commence the service in the dark, but when the trebles sing 'Now Light 1000 Christmas Lights' all the Christmas tree, eve and external lights are switched on simultaneously for a very emotional effect.

Our hidden garden at the Duchess of Kent House is a place of peace, contemplation and sometimes tears, but it is a place of joy and comfort too.

George Solly, Editor

Acknowledgements

This book would never have got off the ground without the help of many people. I would like to thank all those who submitted articles, tips, photographs, drawings and paintings. Also to Mary V Butler, my ever resourceful assistant for proof-reading the entire text.

Picture Credits:
Amber Death	front cover
Miss E Westall	pp 35, 38-9, 43 & rear cover
Gill Howgego	p 42
Graham Rolfe	pp 46-47
George Solly	pp 47, 50 and 95
Ralph Solly	pp 57, 63, 79 and 89
Crocus.co.uk	p 50 (blue)

Plus photographs of celebrities supplied by their agents.

We acknowledge with grateful thanks the financial contribution made by individuals and companies who have helped considerably with the printing costs of this book, in particular:

McKay Securities Group &
Whitewater Nursery & Plant Centre

Amber Death, whose photograph on the front cover won the competition held in support of this book wrote, 'My father, Stephen, was cared for at the Duchess of Kent House in the autumn of 2003. I will always remember how the wonderful staff cared for him at such a personal level.' Steve Death was goalkeeper at Reading Football Club. Steve will remain in the record books for his unbeaten league record of 1103 minutes without conceding a goal while playing for the Royals. Steve was the first choice goalkeeper throughout the '70's after being signed in 1969. Latterly, Steve worked at The Club at Mapledurham as green keeper and is sorely missed. Chosen as the Golf Captains' Charity in 2004, The Club raised a magnificent sum for Duchess of Kent House Trust.
The Editor.

DISCLAIMER
All information contained in this book was believed to be correct at the time of going to print. The publisher accepts no liability for recipes, advice or suggestions made and all submissions have been accepted in good faith for the benefit of the charity.

Duchess of Kent House is a Specialist Palliative Care Centre (in- and out-patient & day therapy) enhancing the quality of life of patients in Reading, central and west Berkshire. The aim of palliative care is to provide holistic and multi-disciplinary specialist treatment focusing on quality of life and the alleviation of distressing symptoms.
Duchess of Kent House Trust is delighted to be associated with and encourage the publication of this *Blooming Famous* gardening and recipe book.

Through the kind support of many, this publication is a valuable fundraiser. Our first venture in this series was *Deliciously Famous* published in 2002 which was a sell-out, netting the charity over £4000. The Trust uses its income to fund or support the following services at Duchess of Kent House: psychologists, aromatherapists, the family support service, the chaplain, the dietician, patient transport, and the provision of equipment and aids. Currently the charity also pays for two in-patient specialist palliative care beds in the centre which are not funded by the NHS at a cost of approximately £93,000 each per year. *In total our need is to find £1000 a day every day of the year!*

By buying this book you have already helped us, for which I thank you most sincerely on behalf of the Trustees. Enjoy the book whether you have green fingers or not. I know I did!

George Solly, Fundraising Manager,
Duchess of Kent House Trust,
22 Liebenrood Road, Reading RG30 2DX.
☎ 0118 939 4889   📠 0118 951 2692
✉ george.solly@duchessofkenthouse.org.uk
www.duchessofkenthouse.org.uk
Charity registration number: 1085912

Conversions

Weights

30g	1oz	150ml	¼ pint
55g	2oz	300ml	½ pint
85g	3oz	450ml	¾ pint
115g	4oz / ¼ lb	600ml	1 pint
225g	8oz /½ lb		
340g	12oz /¾ lb		
450g	16oz /1 lb		
500g	1 lb 2oz		
1kg	2¼ lb		

Temperature

- To convert degrees Celsius into degrees Fahrenheit, multiply by 1.8 and add 32
- To convert degrees Fahrenheit into degrees Celsius, subtract 32 and multiply by 0.55

Length, distance & area

- To convert inches to centimetres, multiply by 2.54
- To convert centimetres to inches, multiply by 0.39
- Feet to metres, multiply by 0.3
- Metres to feet, multiply by 3.28
- Yards to metres, multiply by 0.91
- Metres to yards, multiply by 1.09
- Miles to kilometres, multiply by 1.61
- Kilometres to miles, multiply by 0.62
- Acres to hectares, multiply by 0.4
- Hectares to acres, multiply by 2.47

Weight

- To convert ounces to grams, multiply by 28.35
- To convert grams to ounces, multiply by 0.035
- Pounds to kilograms, multiply by 0.45
- Kilograms to pounds, multiply by 2.21
- British ton to kilograms, multiply by 1016

Volume

- To convert imperial gallons to litres, multiply by 4.55
- To convert litres to imperial gallons, multiply by 0.22

Contents

Blooming Famous - Gardening

Dedication		3
Foreword		5
Acknowledgements		7
Conversion Tables (Gardening)		9
Gardening Tips		12
In Praise of Old Roses	*Fenya Anderson*	16
Dig for Victory	*Angela Barry*	17
A Most Under-Valued Vegetable	*Michael Crawford*	18
Gardening is Full of Surprises	*Jean Garrett*	19
Letter	*Lorraine Kelly*	19
The Night I was Invaded by Cows	*Linda Fort*	20
Garden Volunteers	*Jean Garrett*	21
I'll Never Wash Again	*Alan Titchmarsh*	22
The Plant Hunter	*Toby Musgrave*	23
Italian Renaissance Gardens	*Toby Musgrave*	
	Chris Gardner	24
Royal Horticultural Society		26
Our Patron's Garden		28
Gardens to Visit		29
Reading Gardeners		30
Gardening as a Career		31
Gardening for the Disadvantaged		31
Some Garden Centres in Berkshire		32
Some Gardens Centres in Oxfordshire		36
Some Gardens Centres in Hampshire		41
Sollya Heterophylla	*Adrian Whiteley*	49
Some Garden Centres in Buckinghamshire		53

Contents
Blooming Famous - Recipes

Conversion Table		56
Starters / Vegetarian		57
Watercress & Potato Soup	June Whitfield	58
Mint & Cucumber Salad	Richard Briers	59
Crab Mousse	Min Vaughan-Fowler	60
Avocado with Orange	Paul Daniels	61
Vegetable Roesti	Armin Loetscher	62
Main Courses – Sea Food		63
Grilled Squid	Chris Tarrant	64
Filled Anchovy Hearts	Brian Turner	65
Grilled Sea Bass	Alex Ferguson	66
Sea Bass Sardinian Style	Toni Sale	68
Baked Cod	Anna Stevens	69
Grilled Rainbow Trout	Donald Cartwright	70
Main Courses – Other		72
Steamed Baby Chicken	Brian Turner	73
Ragout of Lamb	Tony Blair	74
Chicken Enchiladas	Bill Clinton	76
Rib of Beef	Jenny Pitman	78
Desserts		79
Transkei Mud	Cliff Richard	81
Crème Brulée	Julie Carr	82
Athol Brose Dessert	John Madejski	83
Rich Chocolate Ice Cream	Terry Wogan	85
Paradise Pudding	Joanna Lumley	86
Stuffed Pears	Jenny & Jim Mason	87
Cakes, Biscuits & Preserves		89
Shirl's Coffee Time Favourite	Shirley Ford	90
Rich Fruit Cake	Suzanne Goodin	91
Preserved Ginger Cake	Delia Smith	92
Dee's Awesome Flapjacks	Matthew Pinsent	94
Celebration Cake	Paul Farmer	95
Blackberry & Apple Jam	Gill Johnson	96
Chocolate Chip Cookies	Nadia Black	97
Making a Donation		98

Gardening Tips

Tip number 1: Squirrels
Squirrels really love digging up my bulbs and chicken wire over the bulbs doesn't seem to deter them. One idea is to get very cheap soap from a supermarket (Asda do an appropriately green one for just a few pence), grate it over the top and stop the little blighters. The only draw back is when it rains...

Oriana Macleod, Trainee Nurse

Tip number 2: Dogs
Fed up with dogs fouling your garden? Then get an empty 2 litre mineral water bottle, fill it with tap water and lie the filled bottle on the ground in the problem area. I don't know why but it seems to work.

'Blackee'. St Anthony's Irish Football Club, Reading

Tip number 3: Pruning
My mother said you should get your worst enemy to prune your roses, as you must be drastic! Prune Hybrid Tea Roses and Floribundas to 23cm high – preferably in March.

Ann Parker, Ward Volunteer.

Tip number 4: Dry Weather
In dry or excessively dry weather dig a 15 – 30 cm trench round garden shrubs; fill the surrounding trench with newspaper well-soaked in water (bath, washing up water etc), replace soil. This one-off treatment will last for some 10 days and ensure shrubs do not die. If heat continues or reoccurs just keep adding water.

Roger Redfern, Ward Volunteer

Tip number 5: Skimmed Milk
I have an organic tip that I find works well. Spraying skimmed milk on your roses at two weekly intervals almost entirely eliminates blackspot. Don't ask me why it works – it just does!

Lucy Summers

Tip number 6: Fruit Trees

Cheer up a small boring back garden by planting cordon, espalier or fan trained fruit trees in front of fence panels. You can have apple, pear, plum, peach, damson fig and many more. They will provide blossom in spring, some fruit in the autumn and they will also hide those panels.

Fred Thompson

Tip number 7: Logs

Logs chopped from felled trees blend well into any garden and are useful in many ways.

You can stand ornamental pots on logs to give extra height, especially in a group arrangement, and in flower beds. Any decayed logs are attractive containers for flowerpots. Good logs can be hollowed out one end enough to contain soil and small plants.

Always stand logs on paving stones to prevent rolling and they will last many years. If bark peels off the trunk, wood can be treated with a preservative.

They are not easy to come by; look for tree felling and expect to buy and pay for delivery. Logs are heavy and difficult to manipulate. I find 1 foot by 3 in diameter and one foot in depth adequate in small gardens.

Evelyn Aust.

Tip number 8: Parsnips

Sowing parsnips in a small garden? To economise on space, sow parsnips a foot apart, and thin to one seedling when appropriate. Halfway between each sowing place 2 or 3 Little Gem lettuce seeds, and thin these down to one seedling when large enough. Your tasty crop of neat lettuces will mature and be enjoyed long before the parsnips need the extra space.

Elizabeth Cockitt

Tip number 9: Fast Food

Banana skins rot down surprisingly quickly – so instead of tossing them onto the compost heap, wait until they blacken and then fork them round the base of your roses. Roses will welcome this 'fast food.'

Betty Lustall

Tip number 10: Soap

Before weeding scrape fingers nails through a bar of soap. This helps to remove soil when washing your hands after weeding.

Carys Thomas

Tip number 11: Tidy Edges

Tidy edges to your lawn will make all the difference. For a straight edge stand on a plank of wood and use a half-moon edger to make a well defined line. For curves mark out the shape with string or a hose pipe. A half-moon edger is much better than using a spade which leaves a scalloped effect.

Len Colvin

Tip number 12: Restoring Wooden Garden Furniture

These volunteers have done a wonderful job restoring wooden garden furniture at Duchess of Kent House. What you will need:
Small roll of sandpaper and sandpaper block
Good quality water based paint brushes
Ronseal or similar 5 year woodstain (we used Mahogany – other shades to choice)
Change into old clothes – rubbing down can be hard on the hands so use gloves.

Make sure wood is clean and dry. Remove any loose wood fibres by sanding. A mini sander might be useful. Two coats of stain were applied. Clean brushes with detergent and water.

Margaret and John Reynolds,
Volunteer gardeners, DoKH

Tip number 13: Book of Days

I recommend keeping a garden diary that goes on through the years. You note, for example, when a particular tree comes into leaf, when you give the lawn its first cut, when seeds are planted and how vegetables crop.

Unseasonable weather and world events add interest, not forgetting family news – perhaps the birth of a grandchild!

It is fascinating to look back as the years roll by.

Paddi Lilley

Tip number 14: Manure
Contact your local riding stables for well rotted horse manure. Often free to the collectors but take your own bags and prepare for a stinky car for days to come!

George Solly.

Tip number 15: Orchids
Watering orchids need not be a problem: once a week put the potted plant in a bowl of tepid water and leave for just 5 minutes. Remove and let drain for a further 5 minutes – simple as that!

Patrick Curtin, Volunteer Gardener at Duchess of Kent House

Tip number 16: Cats
Ground pepper powdered around the base of favoured plants will deter cats!

Helen Easby, Ward Volunteer at Duchess of Kent House

Tip number 17: Slugs
- Halved empty grapefruit peel, turned upside down and placed near vulnerable plants will attract slugs. Inspect under the grapefruit daily and collect slugs for disposal. Melon skins also work well.
- Human hair around plants is said to work as a deterrent (start saving it from your brush and comb!)
- A few drops of oil of pine near a plant (keep off skin)
- Beer in small containers sunk into the ground. At least the slugs drown happily!
- Go out into your garden armed with a torch and you will be amazed how many slugs and snails are about, especially if it is wet. Scoop them up and dispose of as you think fit.
- Encourage wildlife into your garden and try to garden organically to avoid harming wildlife. Birds, frogs, beetles and slow worms all eat slugs and snails. Above all, try not to use toxic slug pellets which can poison not only other wildlife but pets and children too.

Jean Garrett, Garden Volunteer co-ordinator at Duchess of Kent House

In Praise of Old Roses

When I moved to my present garden in Bradfield I replaced an old neglected tennis court with a garden of 19th and early 20th century roses. The soil where the court had been proved to be heavy clay which roses love. I planted some 150 roses in groups of Chinas, Bourbons, Hybrid Musks, Hybrid Perpetuals, Centifolias and Gallicas. An often-repeated criticism of old roses is that they all only flower once. This is completely untrue. Although some varieties do give you just one brilliant show in late spring or summer and then are over for the season, other roses continue to flower until the autumn. One of the most reliable is Comte de Chambord, a luscious pink Portland rose dating from 1860. Another favourite of mine is the old moss rose, Alfred de Dalmas (syn. Mousseline 1855) a white rose with a blush of pink. It produces its delicately beautiful blooms from June to October. For vivid colour, the deep pink Portland, rose de Rescht, (date unknown) is an excellent choice but if you prefer the understated beauty of white roses, try the Hybrid Musk Prosperity (1919). But never forget the once-flowerers. An outstanding rose like the Centifolia, Fantin Latour (1900), with its glorious clusters of pink petals should always find a place in any garden. In June when the rose garden produces its first flush of blooms and its mixture of delicious scents I always wish that more gardeners and gardening writers would, as I do, sing the praises of old roses.

Fenja Anderson

Dig for Victory

My world was turned topsy-turvy when, as a young girl, I became aware of posters and hoardings exhorting one and all to "Dig For Victory". They were produced at the start of WW2.

I loved our modest suburban garden. There was a wonderful circular lawn, with crazy-paving stepping-stones, which was surrounded by borders of roses, lupins, antirrhinums and many other cheerful flowers. There was an apple tree that blossomed beautifully every spring promising abundant fruit but producing very few apples. I liked nothing better than to put on my "siren-suit" and little black Wellingtons (all wellies were black in those days) and be wheeled in the heavy wooden wheelbarrow to wherever I was going to "help" in the garden. My father showed me how to sprinkle seeds of marigolds, nasturtiums and snapdragons on to my very own tiny patch. Then they had to be covered up carefully, tamped down and watered using my very own tiny green watering-can. After that it was a question of waiting............ and waiting........ and waiting until that magical day when we could pick some flowers for my mother.

My "help" in the greenhouse was also welcomed. I learnt how to pinch out the side-shoots of tomato plants and was able to stir their liquid feed very efficiently. Each morning we tramped down the garden to open the windows and each evening they had to be closed. Occasionally we had to rescue a little bird that had become trapped inside.

Then came that fateful day! Thanks to Hitler, householders were urged and encouraged to "Dig For Victory" and produce as much home-grown food as possible. Our lovely lawn was dug up, shrubs were uprooted. The apple-tree was chopped down. My very own little garden disappeared. A lot of back-breaking effort went into digging, raking, riddling and manure spreading. Unexciting rows of potatoes were planted, then carrots, beetroots, lettuces, sprouts etc. And again the waiting began.............. Sad to say, our harvest was never safely gathered in! Suddenly and unexpectedly my father had to take charge of a large group of Liverpool schoolchildren who were being evacuated to Caernomion. Fortunately we were all able to accompany him and we lived in an isolated house out along the wild Welsh coastline of Abershore. The house was completely surrounded by thick gravel so further efforts to "Dig For Victory" had been thwarted. In order to supplement our meagre wartime rations we turned to the sea. We dug in the sand for the fat worms to use as bait on our hooks and lines. Instead of being able to "Dig for

Victory" we were able instead to "Fish for Victory" with very rewarding an immediate results.

Angela M Barry
(Volunteer at Duchess of Kent House)

From Michael Crawford OBE

A Most Under-Valued Vegetable

I always found that stinging nettles are a most under-valued vegetable! During my 'Good Life' years, where I tried to emulate the series by living off the land at my cottage in Bedford, I tried most things. Actually my children tried most things too – usually disguised in one form or another. This particular experiment did not go unnoticed however. The rest of the Sunday roast was eaten with no trouble at all. I had already noticed the surreptitious looks my daughters were giving each other across the kitchen table. I pretended not to notice and tried not to giggle. Doing the honourable thing I ate mine. A slightly furry taste but no sting and the iron content definitely had an effect on my performance in 'Billy' the following week! The children however were made to stay at the table till they had eaten everything on their plates.. This lasted till they were due to go home to their mother. I noticed a few days later that the tomato ketchup bottle was completely empty....my wife called me – I wasn't allowed to see the girls again till I had promised not to feed them stinging nettles again; it was just one vegetable step too far!

Gardening is Full of Surprises

Gardening is full of surprises. The failures make a gardener philosophical, the successes bring delight. Sometimes, against all the odds, truly remarkable things happen. Take the compost heap, for instance.

Over the years, my compost heap has turned up several happy surprises. Non-flowering Nerine Bowdenii bulbs, which I had discarded onto the heap, flowered in profusion in their new home. A beautiful fuchsia plant appeared covered in bloom, presumably from a discarded seed head, and at the present time I have a non-hardy cyclamen plant in bloom poking out between the slats at the side of the heap.

The story I like best, is that of my brother-in-law's peach tree. One day, he found a discarded peach stone sprouting on his compost heap. He potted it up and then grew it on in his greenhouse. In a few years, he had a magnificent tree which produced many luscious, large white peaches. Sadly, due to ill health, he and my sister were forced to move house and so leave the tree behind. The new owners were delighted with the peach tree and the fruit it produced, and called one day to say how delicious they were. Unfortunately, they did not think to bring some with them for Peter and his wife.

Jean Garrett
(Volunteer at Duchess of Kent House)

From Lorraine Kelly

Dear George

I love pottering about in the garden.

We are lucky to get little deer in the back garden as well as pheasants and squirrels.

I really enjoy bird watching and put out food every morning At the moment there's a lovely jay that comes to visit every day!

Lots of love Lorraine Kelly

The Night I was Invaded by Cows!

Less than a month before my father died I sat beside his sickbed and together we took an imaginary walk around the garden of my childhood.

We were able to recall and visualise every plant in the border, every shrub in the boundary hedge throughout the one and a half acre garden. My father was astonished that I could remember the garden so clearly.

I was moved and amazed that we were having the longest and most animated conversation that I could ever remember. It was a touching and poignant day and it is my rather sad little gardening story.

Your gardening stories are probably funnier and much more exciting. If they are, the Duchess of Kent House Trust would like to hear them. The trust is compiling a gardening book this year to raise funds for the hospice charity. Celebrity garden stories, growing tips, information about local gardens and specialist nurseries, hints and aids for disabled gardeners and recipes for home-grown vegetables and fruit will all be gratefully received for the publication – provisionally titled Blooming Famous.

George Solly, fundraising manager at the hospice in Liebenrood Road, West Reading, has a quirky gardening anecdote of his own. The Sollya Heterophylla or Australian Bluebell was named after his ancestor Richard Horsman Solly, a plant physiologist, in around 1830. *(See article on page 48, Ed)*

My most dramatic gardening story happened in the 1980's when a strange woman banged on my conservatory doors late at night. With wild hair and mad staring eyes, she said her cows had escaped from the bottom field into the road and she had been forced to herd them into the only safely enclosed space nearby – my garden. Seven enormous creatures were trampling around in the darkness.

With me bringing up the rear, we cajoled, hallooed and ushered the lowing, meandering monsters out of my garden – by way of all the flower beds down a drive, through a hedge and finally into the right field and safety.

Next morning the garden looked like a waterhole recently visited by a herd of wildebeest. The lawn was pockmarked across its entire surface with deep boreholes filled with muddy water. Shrubs were smashed and border perennials crushed. Cowpats were collected in payment for the damage and put on the compost heap.

The biggest success in the garden the following spring were cowslips, planted the previous summer and growing where the interlopers did most damage.

Linda Fort, Reading Evening Post (first published in Reading's daily paper in 2004) Linda is their gardening and general reporter and publishes an article every Friday in the paper. Linda's gardening highlight of the year is reporting on the annual Reading in Bloom competition held each summer.

Garden Volunteers
Jean Garrett

Gardening at Duchess of Kent House is done almost entirely by a dedicated group of about 10 volunteers who are all keen gardeners and give of their own time on a regular basis.

Originally planted by Lady Palmer's gardener the garden is now looking lovely with new features completed and some others in the pipeline. We have two new water features; one in a raised bed surrounded by a pebble garden, and the other larger one generously donated to us. Another donation was a large greenhouse (given by a local golf club) which our day patients enjoy very much. They grow bedding plants and tomatoes which cropped well last year.

A major set back occurred in 2004 with the building of many new houses on what had been large gardens to the east of our site. However, a new planting scheme has been drawn up and the first screening plants planted in November of 2004.

A new automatic watering system was installed in the same year to water 22 hanging baskets- saving much time and effort.

In summer 2004 we had our first Garden Open Day which we hope to repeat each year in June.

Current plans include the replanting of two raised beds, a new path, plus the introduction of more plants from our 'wish list.'

Our aims for the garden remain constant; it is to be a place of beauty, tranquillity, comfort and to appeal to the senses with perfumed plants, birdsong and the sound of bubbling water.

Jean Garrett, Garden Volunteer Co-ordinator, Duchess of Kent House

I'll Never Wash my Hands Again!

In the days of "Breakfast Time", when the red sofa ruled supreme, I'd just finished a 'live' gardening item, during which I was extolling the virtues of manure, having taken along a bucket of the stuff and pushed my hands into it to show how crumbly and delectable it was. The Programme credits rolled, I started to scrape this wonderful brown soil enrichment from my hands, only to hear the Programme Producer saying to some unseen person: "Don't shake hands with him, you've seen where they've been."

I looked up in time to see The Princess of Wales walking towards me with hands outstretched. We met with a gentle squidge and, as our hands parted, the only thing I could think of to say was "I'll never wash again".

from Alan Titchmarsh

Alan Titchmarsh

From Toby Musgrave

The Plant Hunters

Every week millions tune into gardening programmes and visit garden centres, but how many of us are aware that most of the plants we routinely grown were introduced into this country by a group of determined and brave botanist explorers, who risked (and occasionally gave) their lives exploring and collecting in some of the world's most remote and inhospitable regions.

The father figure of modern plant hunting was Sir Joseph Banks (1743-1820) who sailed with Captain Cook in 1768 on his epoch-making voyage. He subsequently developed Kew into the world's foremost botanic garden and dispatched collectors to all corners of the globe. With Bank's death Kew entered a decline and the plant hunting baton passed to the (later Royal) Horticultural Society. David Douglas (1798-1834) was dispatched to America's Pacific North West, where he survived encounters with hostile Indians and a near drowning, and walked over 9,000 miles on his two expeditions. Douglas discovered over 200 new species including many conifers, and met an untimely end - gored to death by a bull on Hawaii.

By the mid-19th century, the commercial implications of plant hunting were being realised by the Veitch Nursery, Europe's largest, which dispatched 22 hunters between 1840 and 1899. The first two were Cornish brothers. William Lobb (1809-1863) explored South America and California (1840-'64) bringing back the Monkey Puzzle (*Araucaria araucana*) and Giant Redwood (*Sequoiadendron giganteum*). Thomas (1811-1894) searched the jungles of South East Asia (1843-57) for hot house plants to feed the new fashion for conservatories. The last, Ernest Wilson (1876-1930), went to Sichuan, China to find the elusive Handkerchief Tree (*Davidia involucrata*). Despite fever, arrested as a suspected spy and near ship-wreck, he returned thrice more, and on his final expedition (1910-12) to collect the Regal lily (*Lilium regale*) suffered a crushed leg in a landslip.

Sir Joseph Hooker (1817-1911) was the first westerner to enter the Himalayan kingdom of Sikkim in 1847. His spectacular finds kick-started 'rhododendromania', and his unlawful imprisonment provoked annexation. This land was cultivated with tea (*Camellia sinensis*) brought from China by Robert Fortune (1813-1880), the first to properly explore this plant rich land between 1843 and 1859. Renowned for his use of disguise, he was nevertheless robbed, beaten up, and fought a gun battle with pirates. His gift to the garden includes winter flowering gems including *Lonicera fragrantissima*, *Jasminum nudiflorum*, and three mahonias.

The last two great explorers - George Forrest (1873-1932) and Frank Kingdon-Ward (1885-1958) also explored China, but this time Yunnan. The former discovered over 300 *Rhododendron* species, and of all perilous escapes his was the most dramatic. Barefoot, he was chased by murderous Tibetan lamas for three weeks, and without food for nine days, he escaped by scaling a 14,000 ft mountain. Kingdon-Ward made 25 expeditions between 1909 and 1955, and for his part survived fever, a hut collapsing on him, and falling off two precipices. On the second occasion his descent was checked by a bamboo that impaled his armpit. Of his many introductions the stunning blue Himalayan poppy *Meconopsis betonicifolia* is perhaps the most beautiful.

Italian Renaissance Gardens

For half a millennium Italian Renaissance Gardens have influenced garden makers around the world, and the surviving examples stand as monuments to the innovative designers, sculptors, architects, and engineers who built them. Today, however, the gardens tend to be seen only in terms of artful terracing, beautiful statuary, fantastic water works, and large evergreen trees. This is far from the whole story, and to understand these gardens it is essential to get into the Renaissance mind.

Beginning with early 15th century Florence, moving to 16th century Rome, and culminating with the 17th century gardens surrounding the Northern Lakes, Italian Renaissance Gardens were part of a new world order. At its core was a fresh way of thinking that effected a profound reconsideration of the relationship between God, Nature, and Man. The world was now perceived as hierarchical, but with each part interrelated. At the top was God, who had created Man, and Nature. Man perceived the natural world in terms of its usefulness to his needs: plants and animals provided medicine, food, and clothing. Yet at the same time Nature was part of the divinely created cosmos, and so to understand Nature was to further understand God. The garden realm was one in which the subtle interplay and interaction between human culture, the natural world, and the divine cosmos was expressed at its most subtle and complex. Here developed a symbiotic relationship between Man's artistic inventiveness and Nature's diversity and subtlety, which saw their union into an undistinguishable whole, created equally by both, which also offered scope for a symbolic display of the owner's power and wealth.

The Renaissance garden was enclosed with walls, often covered with climbers and fruit trees. But the most important structural elements were the garden's axial arrangement to the house – that is to say a main line ran from the main doorway in the centre of the house to the end of the garden; with areas to right and left of this line essentially mirror images. And its use of terracing - coming off this main axis at right angles, terraces provided cross axes that divided the garden into regular subdivisions. The terraces provided the setting for many of the features that survive – the grottoes, statues, sculptures and spectacular water features, as well as those that have perished - gazebos, pavilions, and groves.

Latticework or pergolas were used to cover the paths and give a stronger visual structure, and the compartments were further subdivided with cross paths to produce a geometric grid pattern of regular units, most commonly squares. These *compartimenti* were defined by a low lattice fence or an herb hedge (lavender, sage, rosemary), which could be ornately arranged in a sort of knot garden design. Each *compartimenti* was planted either with a single specimen, or mixed planting to increase the flower season, and by the 16th century collecting new plants was a widespread obsession. Growing a wide range of rare plants not only displayed the diversity of God's wonders, it simultaneously demonstrated one's wealth.

Sadly, the perishable parts of the gardens have mostly vanished, but several wonderful gardens have survived, notably Villa d'Este (Tivoli), Villa Lante (Bagnaia), Villa Farnese (Caprarola) and the bizarre Bomartzo (Viterbo), which so influenced Salvador Dali.

The Authors

Mr Chris Gardner and Dr Toby Musgrave graduated with Honours degrees in Horticulture from the University of Reading in 1990. Mr Will Musgrave, Toby's younger brother, graduated from the University of Bristol in 1996 with an Honours degree in Archaeology. Chris, with his expert plant knowledge has worked as a Landscape Officer and a freelance garden designer. Toby first lectured in Landscape Horticulture before returning to Reading to study for a doctorate in garden history, a subject he lectures on widely. Chris and Toby formed Gardner Musgrave Associates in 1995, a company which specialises in garden/landscape design and restoration. Work includes the design for Rick Stein's hotel garden in Padstow and the restoration of the 57-acres of The Lost Gardens of Heligan which is being screened this spring as part of a Channel 4 series. Will joined the team in 1996 and concentrates on the research and writing aspects. The combined talents of Chris, Toby and Will have created a dynamic and experienced team. With youth and enthusiasm on their side they share a passion to see gardening in the media injected with vitality. © Copyright 1997 JTT Musgrave, WAS Musgrave & CM Gardner

The Royal Horticultural Society

A passion for plants is what the Royal Horticultural Society is all about, and gardening is a most therapeutic activity.

For 200 years, the RHS has encouraged an interest from people of all ages in gardening and growing plants. This is done through the four RHS gardens (Wisley, Rosemoor, Hyde Hall and Harlow Carr); by publishing inspirational books and gardening magazines; with the splendid Lindley Library; through scientific and educational programmes; and by organising a series of excellent flower shows.

Of these, the Chelsea Flower Show is the best known, and acknowledged throughout the world. Millions of people watch the BBC television programmes about Chelsea, and tens of thousands flock to the show every year. Such is the popularity of the event that it has become rather crowded and the RHS, without increasing overall numbers, is extending the show by an extra day in 2005 to include a Saturday for the first time.

In the meantime, I am reminded of an occasion when two staunch supporters of the show - ladies of a certain age, and not very tall - were braving the throng. One was overheard saying to the other, "You know, dear, they'd get more people here if it wasn't so crowded".

Sir Richard Carew Pole

President, Royal Horticultural Society

RHS gardens to visit

RHS Garden Rosemoor
Great Torrington
North Devon
EX38 8PH
Visit **Rosemoor** at any time of the year and you will find a garden that stimulates all the senses. From Lady Anne's unique and delightful original garden to the new Shrub Rose Garden, Rosemoor Garden provides plenty of ideas and inspiration to take away with you.

RHS Garden Hyde Hall
Rettendon
Chelmsford,
Essex
CM3 8ET
Hyde Hall is a palate of sumptuous rich and varied colours providing inspiration for the novice or keen gardener alike. Just 40 miles from London, this haven of peace and tranquility provides the perfect day out.

RHS Garden Harlow Carr
Crag Lane
Harrogate
North Yorkshire
HG3 1QB
Over the last twelve months, the garden has seen many exciting new developments whilst retaining its uniquely tranquil and welcoming atmosphere. Probably the most spectacular are the 'Gardens through Time' - seven fascinating historical gardens offering a unique living encyclopedia of 200 years of gardening history.

RHS Garden Wisley
Woking
Surrey
GU23 6QB
Whatever the season, with 97 hectares of glorious garden, RHS Garden Wisley demonstrates British gardening at its best. For over 100 years the garden has been a centre of gardening excellence with visitors benefiting from the knowledge and experience of experts. Today you will find that Wisley offers countless inspirational opportunities to gather new gardening ideas.

Become a member of the RHS

Join the RHS today & save £4
For everyone with an interest in gardening
Membership of the RHS allows you to enjoy free entry with a guest to RHS gardens, including Wisley in Surrey, free access to over 120 RHS recommended gardens*, privileged entry and reduced rate tickets to RHS flower shows including Chelsea and Hampton Court Palace, free monthly magazine (RRP £3.95), free comprehensive gardening advice service, access to seeds and much more....

To join for £36 call 0845 130 4646 and quote 2109. (Lines are open Mon-Fri, 9am to 5pm.)

Terms & conditions
The offer is valid until 31/10/05 and cannot be used in conjunction with any other offer or membership transaction. The offer is not available to existing RHS members. Please allow 28 days to receive your membership card and handbook. RHS membership is valid for one year. Individual membership is £40 in the first year and includes a one-off £5 enrolment fee.

*Some throughout the opening season, others at selected periods.

Our Patron's Garden

Sir William Benyon, patron of Duchess of Kent House Trust and his wife Lady Benyon have been avid supporters of this charity over the years. Their home, Englefield House is situated west of Reading just off junction 12 of the M4 and only a few miles from Duchess of Kent House. Their garden is well worth a visit (check 0118 930 2221 for opening times*). Englefield House garden was originally laid out in the seventeenth century with terraces and stone staircases built in 1860. The woodland and water garden on the hill above the house was designed and planted in 1936. In 1976 the formal planting and gravel paths were removed form the terrace and a new planting scheme was put in place with the assistance of Lanning Roper.

* At the time of writing the gardens are open every Monday throughout the year, and on Monday to Thursday from 1st April to 1st November.

Gardens to Visit

Local - Thames Valley

The Living Rainforest, Wyld Court, Hampstead Norrey's
Sir Harold Hillier Gardens, Romsey
Englefield House
The Old Rectory, Burghfield
The Vyne (N.T.) near Basingstoke
Blenheim Palace, Woodstock
Chelsea Physic Garden
Dorneywood (N.T.)
Cliveden (N.T.)Taplow
Greys Court (N.T.) near Henley
Mottisfont Abbey Gardens, Romsey
Wisley Gardens (R.M.S.)
Waddesdon Manor (N.T.) near Aylesbury
West Green House Garden (N.T.)
Waterperry Gardens, Wheatley near Oxford
Wilton House, near Salisbury
Oxford Botanic Garden
Westonbirt Arboretum
"Thrive" Beech Hill H.Q. Horticultural Therapy
Savill Gardens, near Ascot
Herb Farm, Sonning Common
Abbey House Garden, Malmesbury, Wiltshire

France

Monet's Garden, Giverny
Les Jardins du Chateau de Villandry – known for its terraced gardens, including a water garden, a flower garden with box and yew and an ornamental vegetable garden.
Le Jardin d'Altitude du Haut-Chitelet, Vosges Mountains, Alsace, France
Parc Floral du Bois des Moustiers, Varengevilles. Mer, near Dunkirk (house designed by Lutyens)
Fondation Ephrussi de Rothschild, Cap Ferrat, near Nice.

Italy

Boboli Gardens, Florence
Tivoli Gardens, Rome

Elsewhere

Royal Botanic Gardens, Sydney
The Botanical Gardens, Singapore
Butchart Gardens, Victoria, British Columbia
Keukenhof Gardens, near Amsterdam
Cesar Manrique Foundation, Lanzarote

Reading Gardeners

Reading and District Gardeners' Mutual Improvement Association is a Victorian founded Association, formed in 1888 as a charity and it is still a charity today.

In their day Suttons, Waterer's and other thriving nurseries, Milwards the shoe shop, Palmers the biscuit makers, Simmonds the brewery, were major players in supporting the Association as were the staff in the Agricultural and Horticultural Departments of Reading University.

Before the 2nd World War, membership was drawn principally from the professional gardeners employed in the many large gardens in the Reading district, like Leighton Park, Calcot Grange, Caversham Court, Coley Park, and Maiden Erleigh. The Association cared for members and their families who became destitute and helped unemployed gardeners, during this period before State Welfare.

After the war privately owned large gardens were sold, they became too costly to maintain, death duties had to be met and few of our young men who did come back from the war wanted to take up gardening.

The Association has adapted and today has about 160 members. These include some professionals in both practical and academic fields of horticulture, but mainly keen *amateur gardeners.*

From October to March we hold fortnightly evening talks of interest to all gardeners, in Oddfellows Hall at the east end of Oxford Road, by Holy Trinity Church. The hall is on two bus routes, the No 17, Wokingham Road/Tilehurst and No 38 Reading Station/Purley. There is street parking for cars or alternatively, for a nominal fee, in the Central Swimming Pool car park off Battle Street.

During the summer months we have some garden visits.

Membership is open to all. Subscriptions are £5.00 per year for single members and £8,00 for a couple. You are, of course, welcome to attend a couple of meetings without commitment to see if Reading Gardeners suits you. Meetings start at 7.30pm and finish about 9.00pm followed by refreshments at a nominal charge. At each winter meeting we have a raffle.

For membership and other enquiries about the Association, please contact Dorothy Knight, Meadoway, Pine Drive, Mortimer, Reading RG7 3SD, Telephone 0118 933 2508.

Gardening as a Career

The following websites and telephone numbers are helpful when considering a career in horticulture:
The Growing Careers partnership at www.growing-careers.com
The Society of Garden Designers on 01865 301523 or www.sgd.org.uk
The Department for Environment, Food and Rural Affairs (DEFRA) on 020 7238 6173 or visit www.defra.gov.uk
The Royal Horticultural Society (Education Dept) on 01483 224234 or visit www.rhs.org.uk

Gardening for the Disadvantaged

There are a number of charities who use gardening as a way of helping those with disabilities. Often the produce and propagated stock is sold on to the public. In the case of Thrive (see following) they provide training, education and therapy

Thrive - Trunkwell Garden Project, , The Geoffrey Udall Centre, Beech Hill, Reading RG7 2AT
0118 988 5688 www.thriveorg.uk

Englefield Garden Centre
The Street, Englefield, Theale, Reading, RG7 5ES
0118 9304898

Chestnut Nursery, 75 Kingsland Road, Poole BH15 1TN (SWOP Charity)

Some Garden Centres in Berkshire

Berkshire College Of Agriculture
Wall Place, Burchetts Green, Maidenhead, Berkshire, SL6 6QR
01628 824444

Berrybrook Garden Centre
Henley Road, Playhatch, Reading RG4 9RB Tel: 0118 9484794

Blooms Of Bressingham
Weir Bank, Bray on Thames, Maidenhead, Berkshire SL6 2ED
01628 762795

Blooms of Bressingham
Dorney Court, Dorney, Windsor, Berkshire SL4 6QP
01628 669999

Braywick Heath Ltd
41 Braywick Road, Maidenhead, Berkshire, SL6 1DW
01628 22510

Countrywide Farmers Plc
Farm & Country Store, London Road, Twyford, Reading RG10 9EQ
0118 9403770

Cottismore Garden Centre
Newbury Road Kingsclere Newbury Berkshire
01635 298368

Englefield Garden Centre
The Street, Englefield, Theale, Reading, RG7 5ES
0118 9304898

Garden Supplies
Wash Common Post Office & Stores, 59/61 Essex Street, Newbury, Berkshire
RG14 6RA
01635 40587

Grovelands Garden Centre
166 Hyde End Road Shinfield Reading RG2 9ER
01189 884 882 Fax: 0118 9883453

Hillier Garden Centre
Priors Court Road Hermitage Newbury Berkshire RG18 9TG
01635 200 442

Henry Street Garden Centre
Swallowfield Road Arborfield Reading
0118 976 1223 Fax: 0118 9761417

Kennedy's Garden Centre
Floral Mile Hare Hatch Twyford Berkshire
0118 940 3933

Kennedy's Garden Centre
Cedar Cottage Crown Lane, Farnham Royal Slough Berkshire SL2 3SG
01753 647 392

Kennedy's Garden Centre Ltd
Kennedy House 11 Crown Row Bracknell Berkshire RG12 0TH
01344 860022

L.A.D.D. LTD
Hare Hatch Holdings, Bath Road, Hare Hatch, Reading, Berkshire RG10 9SB
Tel: 0118 9404404

Lakeside Garden Centre
Brimpton Common Road, Brimpton Common, Berkshire RG7 4RT
0118 9814138

Moss End Garden Centre
Moss End, Warfield, Bracknell, Berkshire RG12 6EJ
Tel: 01344 483488

Ruralcrafts Garden Centre
374 Reading Road Winnersh Wokingham Berkshire RG11 5EJ
0118 979 0000

Squires Garden Centre
Maidenhead Windsor Berkshire SL4 5UB
01753 865 076

Scats Countrystore
Kiln Road Shaw Newbury Berkshire RG13 2HH
01635 43436

Percy Stone Ltd
4-8 Reading Road, Pangbourne, Reading, RG8 7LY
0118 9842111

Stubbings Nursery
Stubbings Estate, Henley Road, Maidenhead, Berkshire, SL6 6QL
01628 825454

West East Trading
Ladds Garden Village, Bath Road, Hare Hatch, Reading, Berks RG10 9SB
0118 940 4794

William Wood & Son Ltd
The Bishop Centre, Bath Road, Taplow, Maidenhead, Berkshire SL6 0NY
01628 605454

Woodcote Nursery & Garden Centre
Woodcote, Reading, Berkshire RG8 0QX
01491 680335

Wyevale Garden Centre
Forest Road Binfield, Bracknell Berks, RG42 4HA
01344 869456

Wyevale Garden Centre
Cedar Cottage, Crown Lane Farnham Royal Slough, Berks, SL2 3SG
01753 645627

Wyevale Garden Centre
Floral Mile, Hare Hatch Twyford, near Reading
RG10 9SW
0118 940 3933

Wyevale Garden Centre
4a Bath Road Hungerford Berkshire, RG17 0HE
01488 682916

Wyevale Garden Centre
Heathlands Road Wokingham Berks. RG40 3AS
0118 9773055

Kaffa Lily

Wyevale Garden Centre
Dedworth Road Windsor Berkshire, SL4 4LH
01753 841791

Wyevale Garden Centre Bath Road Thatcham Berkshire, RG18 3AN
01635 871760

Yew Tree Garden Centre Ball Hill East Woodhay Newbury Berkshire
RG20 0NG
01635 255 250

Some Garden Centres in Oxfordshire

Bicester Garden Centre
Oxford Road Bicester Oxfordshire OX6 8NY
01869 242248

Burford Garden Centre
Shilton Road Burford Oxfordshire OX18 4PA
01993 823117

Charlton Park Garden Centre
Charlton Road Wantage Oxfordshire OX12 8EP
012535 772700

Farnborough Garden Centre
Southam Road Farnborough Banbury Oxfordshire OX17 1EL
01295 690479

Frost Millets Farm Kingston Road Frilford Oxfordshire OX13 5HB
01865 391923

Hurrans Garden Centre
Compton Road Banbury Oxfordshire OX16 8PR
01295 266300

Millets Farm Garden Centre
Abingdon Road Frilford Abingdon
Oxfordshire OX13 5HB
01865 391923

Northleigh Garden Centre
Northleigh Oxford OX7 2AQ
01993 881372

Ridgeway Nursery
The Ridgeway Bloxham Banbury Oxon OX15 4NF
01295 720859

Scats Countrystore
The Old Railway Station Park Road Faringdon
Oxon SN7 7BP
01367 241768

Summertown Garden Centre
200 - 202 Banbury Road Oxford OX2 7BY
01865 554959

Toad Hall Garden Centre
Henley-on-Thames Oxfordshire RG9 3AG
01491 574615

Waterperry Garden
Waterperry Wheatley Oxfordshire OX5 1PA
01844 339226

Wyevale Garden Centre
Newbury Road Chilton, Near Didcot Oxon, OX11
01235 833900

Wyevale Garden Centre Reading Road Henley-on-Thames Oxon RG9 4AE
0118 940 3078

Wyevale Garden Centre Southern By-Pass South Hinksey Oxford OX1 5AR
01865 326066

Wyevale Garden Centre 57 London Road Wheatley Oxford. OX33 1YJ
01865 873057

Yarton Nurseries Sandy Lane Yarton Oxfordshire OX5 1PA
01865 842003

Rugosa Rose

Myrtle

Northleigh Garden Centre
Northleigh Oxford OX7 2AQ
01993 881372

Ridgeway Nursery
The Ridgeway Bloxham Banbury Oxon OX15 4NF
01295 720859

Scats Countrystore
The Old Railway Station Park Road Faringdon
Oxon SN7 7BP
01367 241768

Summertown Garden Centre
200 - 202 Banbury Road Oxford OX2 7BY
01865 554959

Toad Hall Garden Centre
Henley-on-Thames Oxfordshire RG9 3AG
01491 574615

Waterperry Garden
Waterperry Wheatley Oxfordshire OX5 1PA
01844 339226

Wyevale Garden Centre
Newbury Road Chilton, Near Didcot Oxon, OX11
01235 833900

Wyevale Garden Centre Reading Road Henley-on-Thames Oxon   RG9 4AE
0118 940 3078

Wyevale Garden Centre Southern By-Pass South Hinksey Oxford OX1 5AR
01865 326066

Wyevale Garden Centre 57 London Road Wheatley Oxford. OX33 1YJ
01865 873057

Yarton Nurseries Sandy Lane Yarton Oxfordshire OX5 1PA
01865 842003

Some Garden Centres in Hampshire

Abbey Garden Centre
Mill Lane Titchfield Fareham Hampshire PO15 5RB
01329 842 225

Abbey Garden Centre
Southampton Road Cadnam Southampton Hampshire SO32 2AE
01703 812240 Fax: 023 80814186

Arturi's Garden Centre
Allington Lane Fair Oaks Eastleigh Hampshire SO5 7DE
01703 602 234

Avenue Nurseries Garden Centre
The Avenue Lasham Alton Hampshire GU34 5RX
01256 381 648

Afton Garden Centre
Honnor & Jeffrey Afton Road Freshwater Isle of Wight PO40 9UH
01983 752870

Busy Bee Nurseries (IOW) Ltd.
Brading Road Ryde Isle of Wight
01983 811096

Bashley Plant Centre
Bashley Common Road New Milton Hampshire BH25 5SG
01452 612 442

Baily's Garden Centre
Wildmoor Lane Sherfield On Lodden Basingstoke Hants RG27 0HA
01256 882 776

Brambridge Park Garden Centre
Kiln Lane Brambridge Hampshire S050 6HT
01962 713 707

Coach House Garden Centre
London Road (A30), Hartley Wintney, Basingstoke, Hampshire RG27 8HY
01252 842400

Marigold

Autumn Leaves

Conkers Garden Centre
London Road Hatch Nr.Basingstoke HANTS
01256 840515

Coniger Nurseries
Bishopstoke Road Eastleigh Hampshire SO50 6AD
01703 612 385

Country Market
Malthouse & Osborne Farms Kingsclere Hampshire
01420 477582

J ELLIS & SONS BORDON LTD
Headley Mill, Bordon, Hampshire GU35 8RJ
014203 2031

Everton Nurseries
Everton Lymington Hampshire SO41 0JZ
01590 642155

Elm Park Garden Centre & Nursery
Aldermaston Road Pamber End Tadley Hampshire
01256 850587

Exbury Gardens Retail Ltd
The Estate Office, Exbury, Southampton, Hampshire SO45 1AZ
023 80898625

Fairweather Garden Centre
High Street Beaulieu Brokenhurst Hampshire SO42 7YB
01590 612 307

Fairwinds Garden Centre
126 High Street Lymington Hampshire SO41 9AQ
01590 677022

Fontly Nurseries
Fontly Road Titchfield Fareham Hampshire PO15 6QX
01329 844336

Frampton & Sons Ltd
48 High Street, Ringwood, Hampshire BH24 1BQ
01425 472342

G A Day
Burfields Road Portsmouth Hampshire P03 5NA
01705 662261

Garthowen Garden Centre & Nursery
Alton Lane, Four Marks, Alton, Hampshire GU34 5AJ
01962 773225

Goodlife Farm Shop Garden Centre
Springvale Road, Headbourne, Hampshire SO23 7LD
01962 889000

Guys Nurseries
Forest Corner Ringwood Hampshire BH24 3HW
01425 662261 Fax: 01425 470892

S Guy Limited
115 Pyle Street Newport ISLE OF WIGHT PO30 1XA
01983 522094

Hambrooks Garden Centre
135 Southampton Road Titchfield Fareham Hampshire PO14 4PR
01489 572285

Hambrook Garden Centre
Wangfield Lane Curdridge Southampton Hampshire SO3 2DA
01489 780505

Haskins Garden Centre
Gaters Hill, Mansbridge Road, West End, Southampton, Hampshire SO3 3HW
Tel: 023 80472324
Fax: 023 80462217

Hillier Garden Centre
Romsey Road Winchester Hampshire SO22 5DN
01962 842288

Hillier Garden Centre
Jermyns Lane Braishfield Romsey Hampshire SO51 9PA
01794 368407

Hanging Baskets outside In-Patients' Entrance, Duchess of Kent House

Eastern garden of Duchess of Kent House, showing Rose's Garden Room

Garden seating (as restored by volunteers!)

47

Hillier Garden Centre
Woodhouse Lane Botley Hampshire SO3 2EZ
01489 782306

Hillier Garden Centre
Farnham Road, Liss, Hampshire, GU33 6LJ
Tel: 01730 892196
Fax: 01730 893676

Hillier Garden Centre
Botley Road Romsey Hampshire SO51 8ZL
01794 513459

Hilltop Nursery
Beaulieu Hampshire SO42 7YR
01590 612113 Fax: 01590 612615

Home & Garden
Queens Parade, 159 Privett Road, Gosport, Hampshire, PO12 3SS
Tel: 023 92582678
Fax: 023 92582678

Honnor & Jeffrey Ltd.
Dalverton Garden Centre Newport Road Sandown ISLE OF WIGHT PO36
01983 868602

Hook Garden Centre
Reading Road Hook Hampshire RG27 9DB
01256 768700

Jubilee Garden Centre
Newport Road Branstone Sandown ISLE OF WIGHT PO36 00T
01983 865562

Littleton Nurseries
Winchester Hampshire SO22 6QQ
01962 880292

Lugershall Garden Centre
Granby Gardens Lugershall Andover Hampshire SP11 9RG
01264 790275

Sollya Heterophylla- Richard Horsman Solly

The bluebell creeper, as its name suggests, is a slender twining plant found in the wild in Australia, scrambling through shrubs to a height of 2-3 m (6-8ft) or loosely covering the ground at about 30cm (12in).

It is evergreen, with leaves of variable size and shape, hence its name heterophylla, meaning various-leaved. A single plant can look rather different at certain stages of growth or under differing cultural conditions.

The startling sky-blue flowers are its crowning glory, and are freely produced from April to September. The flowers are shaped like the skirt of a crinoline ball gown, with a minute calyx and five board, overlapping petals about 1cm long. Each petal can reportedly be peeled into two layers, like a 2 ply tissue.

For those in the UK, it is a delicate shrub ideally needing greenhouse protection, however, in sheltered urban gardens or warmer areas of the UK it can survive outside, scrambling through an evergreen shrub or cascading down from the top of a wall.

No-one could fail to be flattered to have a plant named in their honour, but some plants are more attractive than others. Imagine, then, the delight that the British plant physiologist Richard Horsman Solly must have felt in about 1830, when he first saw one of the two species of the genus that was given his name. Sollya Heterophylla. Commonly called the Bluebell Creeper or Australian Bluebell, it is a charming plant.

Extracted from an article by ADRIAN WHITELEY, a botanist at RHS Garden Wisley, UK.
Editor's note:

Having a great interest in my family tree as well as gardening I could not refrain from including this article! I am a direct descendant of Richard Horsman Solly he being of the 12th generation from my start point in 1418 with me the 16th. For some time I tried in vain to find examples of Sollya Heterophylla. Whilst organising our annual Charity Golf Day at nearby Sandford Springs Golf Club I found Wolverton Plants situated at Wolverton Common near Kingsclere to be stockists of all three examples: pink, white and blue. Only the blue is AGM standard. Ring 01635 298453 for stock position before visiting.

Sollya Heterophylla (white)

Sollya Heterophylla (blue)

MJS Garden Centre
Wildmoor Lane Sherfield On Loddon Basingstoke Hampshire RG27 0JD
01256 882239

Prince's Garden Centre
London Road Rake Hampshire GU33 7JH
01730 894011

Pococks Nuseries
Dandy's Ford Lane Sherfield English Romsey Hampshire SO51 6DT
01794 323514

Pococks' Roses
Jermyns Lane, Romsey, Hampshire SO51 0QA
Tel: 01794 367500
Fax: 01794 323514

Redcliffe Gardeners
Bashley Road New Milton Hampshire BH25 5RY
01425 619691

Redfields Garden Centre
Ewshot Lane Church Crookham Fleet Hampshire GU13 0UB
01252 624 444

MA Rose & Son
23 Market Street, Alton, Hants GU 34 1HA
01420 82339

S C A T S Country Store Ltd
134 Weyhill Road, Andover, Hampshire SP10 3BH
01264 323482

S C A T S Country Store Ltd
Easton Lane Winnall Winchester SO23 TRU
01962 863007

S C A T S Country Store Ltd
Canister House, 27 Jewry Street, Winchester SO23 8RY
01962 875200

S C A T S Country Store Ltd
Mount Pleasant Lane, Sway Road, Lymington, Hampshire SO4 9ZS
01590 676633

S C A T S Country Store Ltd
Inharns Road Holybourne Alton Hampshire GU34 4EX
01420 83511

Silver Springs Nursery
Fontley Road, Titchfield, Fareham, Hampshire PO15 6QX
01329 842114

Springfields Nursery
Oakhanger Bordon Hampshire
01420 472 528

Streets
11 East Street, Havant, Hampshire PO9 1AB Tel: 023 92471516

Valley Nurseries (About Plants Ltd.)
Basingstoke Road, Alton, Hampshire GU34 4AB
01420 549700

Vigo Nursery
72 Vigo Road, Andover, Hampshire SP10
01264 323893

Whitewater Nursery & Plant Centre
Hound Green
Hook, Hampshire
0118 932 6487

World Of Water (Romsey)
93 Great Bridge Road, Romsey, Hampshire SO51 OHB
01794 515923

Wyevale Garden Centre
Salisbury Road Andover Hants SP11 7DN
01264 710551

Wyevale Garden Centre
Winchester Road North Waltham, Basingstoke Hants RG25 2DJ
01256 397155

Wyevale Garden Centre
Winchester Road Fair Oak, Eastleigh Hampshire, SO50 7HD
02380 600392

Wyevale Garden Centre
Bartons Road Havant Hants PO9 5NA
02392 456200

Wyevale Garden Centre
Wildmoor Lane Sherfield-on-Loddon Basingstoke Hampshire, RG27 0JD
01256 882239

Some Garden Centres in Buckinghamshire

Booker Garden & Leisure Centre
Clay Lane, Booker, Marlow, Bucks SL7 3DH
01494 532532

Bourne End Garden Centre & Nursery Group
Hedsor Road, Bourne End, Bucks SL8 5EE Tel: 01628 523926

Buckingham Nurseries
28 Tingewick Road Buckingham
MK18 4AE
01280 813556

Countrywide Farmers Plc
Finmere Mill, Tingewick, Buckingham, Bucks MK18 4BR
01280 848551

Flowerland At Bourne End
4-6 The Parade, Bourne End, Bucks SL8 5QQ
01628 521744

Flowerland At Iver
Norwood Lane, Iver, Bucks SL0 0EW
01753 655685

Flowerland At West Wycombe
Chorley Road, West Wycombe, Bucks HP14 3AP
01494 438635

Frosts Garden Centre
Newport Road Woburn Sands Milton Keynes Bucks MK17 8UE
01908 583 511

Fulmer Plant Park Ltd
Cherry Tree Lane, Fulmer, Bucks SL3 6JE
01753 662604

Haddenham Garden Centre
Stanbridge Road Haddenham Nr Aylesbury Bucks HP17 8HN
01844 290395

Hildreths Ltd
169 Wycombe Road, Prestwood, Great Missenden, Bucks HP16 0HJ
Tel: 01494 862720

Jardinerie Limited
Studley Green, Stokenchurch, High Wycombe, Bucks HP14 3UX
01494 483761

South Heath Garden Centre & Nursery Ltd
South Heath, Great Missenden, Bucks HP16 9OH
01494 863269

Springbridge Nurseries
24-26 Oxford Road, Denham, Bucks UB9 4DF
01895 835939

Marlow Garden And Leisure Centre
Pump Lane South Little Marlow
Bucks SL7 3RB
01628 472 922

Wood Lane Nursery & Garden Centre
Wood Lane Iver Heath Buckinghamshire SL0 0LG
01753 653168
E-mail: enquiries@wood-lane-nursery.co.uk

World's End Garden Leisure Centre
Aylesbury Road, Wendover, Bucks HP22 6BD
01296 623116

Wyevale Garden Centre
London Road
Beaconsfield Bucks HP9 1SH
01494 672522

Wyevale Garden Centre
Pump Lane South Little Marlow, Marlow Bucks. SL7 3RB
01628 482716

Wyevale Garden Centre
Aylesbury Road Wendover Aylesbury Bucks. HP22 6BD
01296 623116

Wyevale Garden Centre
Newport Road Woburn Sands Milton Keynes. MK17 8UF
01908 281161

Wyevale Garden Centre
Junction Avebury Boulevard & Secklow Gate Milton Keynes. MK9 3BY
01908 604011

Virtual Garden Suppliers

Crocus
Customers can place orders online at www.crocus.co.uk or call the 24 hour call centre on 0870 7871414

Deliciously Famous

When Deliciously Famous was printed in 2002 it was an immediate success and the original print run of 1200 soon exhausted. We had hoped to bind new copies from the remaining 200 or so sets of pages left by the printer, which was part of his 'over-run'. However, in the meanwhile the printer was moving premises so any printed paper stocks were destroyed to make for easier removal and storage.

We thus had many dozens of disappointed supporters unable to get copies of the Deliciously Famous cookbook. It has therefore been decided to reprise some of these recipes into this book which follow:

Conversions

Oven Temperatures

Celsius	Fahrenheit	Gas	Description
110 °C	225 °F	Mark 1/4	Cool
130 °C	250 °F	Mark 1/2	Cool
140 °C	275 °F	Mark 1	Very low
150 °C	300 °F	Mark 2	Very low
170 °C	325 °F	Mark 3	Low
180 °C	350 °F	Mark 4	Moderate
190 °C	375 °F	Mark 5	Moderately hot
200 °C	400 °F	Mark 6	Hot
220 °C	425 °F	Mark 7	Hot
230 °C	450 °F	Mark 8	Very hot

For those of you with a fan oven reduce temperature by 10 °C or consult manufacturer's handbook.   Tsp = teaspoon   Tbsp = tablespoon

Weights

30g	1oz	150ml	¼ pint
55g	2oz	300ml	½ pint
85g	3oz	450ml	¾ pint
115g	4oz / ¼ lb	600ml	1 pint
225g	8oz / ½ lb		
340g	12oz / ¾ lb		
450g	16oz / 1 lb		
500g	1 lb 2oz		
1kg	2¼ lb		

Starters / Vegetarian Dishes

June Whitfield

An elderly duke was asked to be Guest of honour at the county annual dinner. The next day he met a friend who said "Sorry I couldn't get to the dinner last night – how was it?"
"Well, Arthur "said the Duke sighing, I'll tell you about it." If the melon had been as cold as the soup and if the soup had been as warm as the claret and the claret had been as old as the chicken and the chicken had been as young as the waitress and if the waitress had been as willing as the Duchess – I'd have had a jolly good evening".
June Whitfield one of our stars of stage, screen and radio for many years.

Watercress and Potato Soup (Serves 4-6)

Ingredients:
110g / ¼ lb of potatoes scrubbed
2 sticks of celery chopped
1 large onion
1 chicken stock cube or 600ml chicken stock
2 bunches of watercress
50g / 2oz butter and seasoning

Method:
Cut the potatoes into pieces and add to the celery and onion in a large saucepan. Add the butter and sauté until lightly browned. Add stock cube mixed with 600ml water, plus another 1200 ml of water. Add watercress. Cook until potato is soft. Blend in a liquidiser. Season to taste, simmer for 20 minutes. Garnish with croutons, fried onion or a swirl of cream. June tells us that this soup freezes well. It should be thawed overnight in a refrigerator and reheated thoroughly.

Richard Briers

Customer "waiter- what soup is this?
Waiter: "Its bean soup sir"
Customer "I don't want to know what its BEEN - I want to know what it is! ! !

Richard star of The Good Life and more recently Monarch of the Glen has sent a recipe to us from his own cookbook "GROW YOUR OWN NOSH"

Mint and Cucumber Salad (Serves 4)

Ingredients:

1 cucumber
2 small cartons of plain yoghurt
1 teaspoon of chopped mint leaves
1 teaspoon of chopped parsley
1 tomato, quartered
Freshly ground pepper

Method:

Peel the cucumber and dice it very small.
Mix it with the chopped mint leaves and yoghurt.
Sprinkle chopped parsley on top and decorate with tomato quarters.
Sprinkle with freshly ground pepper.
Place in a cool place for an hour before serving.

Min Vaughan-Fowler

Min Vaughan-Fowler is another of our volunteers and has been for the past three years. She comes in on a regular basis, on a Friday, and helps out in our day unit doing a variety of different things with our patients. Min is also a cordon bleu cook and has helped me a great deal with some of the recipes. Friday has become "Min's Cake Day". The patients take turns in choosing the following week's cake. The favourite seems to be her Victoria Sandwich, made with her own farm fresh eggs!

Crab Mousse

A delicious recipe of Min's for seafood fans everywhere!!

Ingredients:
450g / 1lb defrosted or fresh white crab meat
5 tbsp of mayonnaise
Salt and pepper to taste
A dash of Worcestershire Sauce
Squeeze of lemon juice
150 ml / ¼ Pint of double cream

Method:
Mix everything together and put into a soufflé or similar serving dish. Decorate with cucumber slices and a pinch of paprika, chill before serving.

Paul Daniels

George Solly and Suzanne Goodin met Paul Daniels at BBC Radio Berkshire when they were invited to the Breakfast Show by Nicki Whiteman to talk about palliative care and to promote Deliciously Famous. Paul is probably the U.K's most famous T.V magician. He promised to send Suzanne a recipe which he did the very next day.

Avocado with Orange and Grapefruit (Serves 4)

Ingredients:
2 tins of orange and grapefruit segments
1 large avocado
Sprig of mint
Vinaigrette:
1 tbsp olive oil.
1 tbsp white wine vinegar
½ tsp sugar
½ tsp French mustard.

Method;
Chop avocado in large chunks add to drained fruit- chop mint, saving a little for decoration. Stir in vinaigrette. Serving suggestion: add a little vinaigrette dressing and serve on a bed of shredded lettuce in individual dishes.

Armin Loetscher

Armin has run the most successful St Moritz Restaurant in Soho's Wardour Street, W1 for decades. Apart from specialising in the cuisine of his home country – Switzerland – Armin's deceptively spacious premises also accommodates a club in the basement available for special functions.

Vegetable Roesti

Ingredients:
800g waxy potatoes, boiled in their skins the previous day
Salt
4 tbsp butter
1 carrot
¼ cauliflower
½ broccoli
¼ each green, yellow and red pepper (blanch all vegetables)
150g Vachérin Fribourgois cheese

Method:
Peel and coarsely grate the potatoes and season with salt. Heat the butter in a frying pan and add the grated potatoes. Fry gently on one side, then turn over and add cooked vegetables onto potatoes. Sprinkle cheese over vegetables.
Cover pan and fry for a further few minutes until the cheese has melted over the vegetables.

Main Courses - Sea Food

Chris Tarrant

Reading-born Chris Tarrant says "as a fanatical fisherman my favourite dish is of course a fish recipe". This is his favourite recipe for squid as the Kiwi juice makes it very sweet and tender......... He hopes you enjoy it !!!!!

Grilled Squid with Kiwi and Lime Marinade

Ingredients:
Marinade
Squid
Juice of Kiwi fruit
Juice of ½ a Lime
2 tbsp of olive oil
1 clove of garlic, crushed
1 chopped red chilli (optional)
Salt and black pepper

Ask the fishmonger to clean the squid removing the intestines and pen, wash and skin the tentacles if used. Cut the body open to give a large triangle of flesh, with a sharp knife scrape the membrane from the inside of the fish, turning it over to scrape off any skin or membrane from the other side. Make diagonal cuts across the flesh at about ½ inch intervals; do this both ways to give a crossed hatch appearance. Mix all the marinade ingredients together, cut the squid into serving size portions and cover with the marinade, leave for about 30 minutes. Cook under a hot grill for 3 – 4 minutes each side.

'Chris serves this with sauté potatoes and a rocket salad'.

Brian Turner CBE

TV Chef and Restaurateur Brian Turner CBE, heard about our first book from Jon Jon Lucas, the head chef at his London restaurant and very kindly sent three recipes. Two of these recipes not published last time are now included.

Artichoke Heart filled with Crab & Shrimp served in a Tarragon Hollandaise (Serves 4)

Ingredients:
4 large cooked artichoke hearts
115g crab meat
225g shrimps
225g clarified butter
2 egg yokes
2 tbsp chopped tarragon
1 tsp white wine vinegar
salt & pepper
2 tomatoes concasse
300ml clear stock
½ lemon juice
curly endive and dressing

Method:
1. Put hearts in stock to reheat
2. Sweat the crab meat and shrimps together in butter
3. Beat egg yokes over water with lemon juice. Slowly add clarified butter
4. Season and add chopped tarragon
5. Bind crab meat and shrimps with 1 tbsp of sauce
6. Drain off the hearts and fill with the mixture
7. Coat the filled artichoke hearts with sauce
8. Dress curly endive with tomato concasse and olive oil. Salt and pepper
9. Put salad on plate
10. Balance heart on top
11. Serve.

Sir Alex Ferguson

'Manchester United's Manager Sir Alex Ferguson CBE is clearly a pasta and fish fan!!!!! I have tried this recipe and my husband and brother-in-law thoroughly enjoyed it. I did have problems trying to buy the Red Pepper coulis and in the end I had to bring on a substitute.
I used a fresh Mediterranean sauce from Waitrose.' – Suzanne Goodin.

Grilled Sea Bass with Fettuccine and Ratatouille Sauce
(Serves 4)

Ingredients:
450g / 1lb pasta dough
50g / 2 oz unsalted butter
Salt and freshly ground black pepper
4 Sea Bass fillets each about 175- 225g/ 6 -8 oz
25 ml 1 fl oz olive oil

For the Ratatouille Sauce
1 red pepper seeded
1 green pepper seeded
2 shallots
½ aubergine
25g / 1 oz unsalted butter
25 ml Olive oil
300 ml / 10 fl.oz of red pepper coulis
1 courgette

Method:
To make the fettuccine, roll the dough through a pasta machine several times until it is about 1 mm thick, then pass through the noodle cutter and leave to rest (You can substitute with ready-made).

To make the Ratatouille, cut the vegetables into 5 mm slices, melt butter with the olive oil in a large pan, add the vegetables and cook for 3 – 4 minutes until softened. In another pan warm the red pepper coulis, add the vegetables, season with salt and pepper. Pre heat the grill to medium, season and butter a flame proof baking tray. Lay the sea bass fillets onto the prepared tray (Skin side up) and cook under medium grill for about 8 minutes. While the fish is cooking, boil a large pan of water with olive oil and a pinch of salt, when the water is boiling drop in the pasta and move it around with a fork, this will only take a few minutes. Drain through a colander season with salt and pepper and toss with remaining butter to loosen. Warm the ratatouille sauce and spoon it onto hot plates. Sit the fettuccine in the middle and lay the grilled sea bass on the top.

Sir Alex says "I hope you enjoy this dish, as much as I do ….."

Toni Sale

Toni Sale is a well known Reading Restaurateur specialising in Italian and Sardinian specialities. Every year Toni runs a marathon or two to support his favourite charities – he has run recently for Children with Leukaemia and Duchess of Kent House Trust.

Spigola alla Sarda - *(Sea bass Sardinian Style)*

Ingredients – per fish cooked
1 whole sea bass per person – 500g weight approx.
Clove of garlic – crushed
Wedge of lemon
Sprig of fresh dill
Coarse sea salt
Extra virgin olive oil
Method:
Take the fish and gut it, but do not remove the scales
Place the crushed garlic, lemon wedge and dill inside the fish.
Take a baking tray and sprinkle a light layer of sea salt on it, place the fish on top and then completely cover the whole fish with a layer of salt.
Sprinkle a few drops of water on top of the salt and bake in a pre-heated oven (220-230°C / gas mark 7- 8) for 30/35 minutes.
Take the tray with the fish out of the oven and gently scrape the salt off.
Place the sea bass on a serving dish or plate and open it out flat so that the flesh is facing up, then take the bone out.
Sprinkle some extra virgin olive oil on top and your sea bass is ready to eat – enjoy!!
N.B if you are cooking more than one fish, allow a slightly longer cooking time

Dr Anna Stevens

Dr Anna Stevens is a part-time assistant G.P. at The Grovelands Medical Centre, Reading and a busy mother of two.

Baked Cod with an Olive and Bacon Tartar Sauce

Ingredients:
2 Cod Fillets 175g - 225g
2 tbsp Mayonnaise
2 tbsp thick yoghurt (not the set kind)
Handful of canned Black Olives
2 rashers of cooked bacon
Chopped parsley
Knob of butter
Salt and freshly ground black pepper.

Method:
Place the Cod fillets in a roasting tin, dot with butter, season with salt and the freshly ground pepper and cover with a lid or tin foil.

Bake for 20 minutes at 200°C / 400°F Gas Mark 6, until cooked through.

Meanwhile drain and chop the olives, chop the cooked bacon and mix with the mayonnaise and the yoghurt dressing until the desired consistency is reached. Sprinkle with the freshly chopped parsley and pour over the fish. Serve with steamed courgettes and baked potato wedges.

Donald Cartwright

Donald Cartwright is the Executive Head Chef of the popular Reading Restaurant Colley's Supper Rooms. He very kindly sent the following recipe for Grilled Rainbow Trout and Oven sweetened Tomato Galette with Gin and orange cream.

Grilled Rainbow Trout and Oven-Sweetened Tomato Galette with a Gin and Orange Sauce (serves 8)

Ingredients:
8 small rainbow trout fillets (Skin on)
8 ripe plum tomatoes
1 pack / 400g of puff pastry
Small amount of good olive oil
1 bag of green salad leaves
Salt and fresh ground pepper
Butter

For the sauce
100g / 4oz butter
Juice and zest of one orange
Pinch of the corner of a chicken stock cube
2 *pub* measures of gin
3- 4 saffron strands
600 ml/ 1 pint of pourable double cream

Method:
The day before:
slice the tomatoes in half length ways, lay the cut side up on a baking sheet, season and dribble with olive oil, cook until dry but still squishy in the oven on the lowest temperature.
On the day:
Roll out the pastry into rectangles, slightly longer and wider than the trout fillets. Prick with a fork all over to hinder rising. Place on a paper lined baking sheet; add the tomatoes length ways onto the pastries (2 pieces each).

Bake until the sides rise up approximately 15 minutes on medium heat.

For the sauce:
Make this up to 2 hours before eating but do not chill after cooking.

Place all the ingredients except the cream into a saucepan and cook on low until they bind together and look like orange honey. This takes about 5 – 10 minutes. Turn up the heat, add the cream and bring to the boil. Reduce the heat for 2 minutes and simmer until a slightly thicker coating consistency is achieved. Put a lid on the pan and leave until you need it.

Butter and season the fish. Grill the trout fillets skin side up, for about 4 – 5 minutes. When the skin blisters and colours it will be cooked.

Galettes
Warm the galettes in the oven for 2 minutes then arrange on plates.
1. Warm the sauce slowly
2. Place the trout skin side up
3. Gently place onto the centre of your plate
4. Dribble sauce round the edge
5. Place a small pile of leaves on the galette
6. Drizzle over olive oil

Main Courses – Other

Brian Turner CBE

Steamed Baby Chicken with Peppers & Herbs on a bed of Baby Vegetables

Ingredients:
4 baby chickens
1 red pepper
1 tbsp tarragon
1 tbsp parsley
115g butter
225g carrots
225g swede
225g turnip
12 broccoli florets
600ml vegetable stock

Method:

1. Remove wish bone and loosen skin over the chicken breast
2. Chop peppers and sweat in butter, add a little water and cook until soft
3. Puree and add to tarragon and parsley and then mix with butter
4. Push under the skin of the chicken and tie back into original shape
5. Steam for approximately 25-35 minutes depending on size
6. Shape carrots, swede and turnip into barrel shapes
7. Cut broccoli into fleurettes
8. Cook separately in vegetable stock
9. When almost cooked, take out and put into iced water. Refresh, take out and drain
10. When chicken is almost ready, put vegetables around it to reheat thoroughly
11. Take out the chicken, cut into breasts and legs
12. Arrange with a bed of vegetables around a soup plate. Serve.

Tony Blair

10 DOWNING STREET
LONDON SW1A 2AA

From the Direct Communications Unit 28 May 2002

Ms Suzanne G Goodin
Duchess of Kent House Trust
Delwood Community Hospital
22 Liebenrood Road
Reading
RG30 2DX

Dear Ms Goodin

The Prime Minister has asked me to thank you for your recent letter about the recipe book you are compiling.

Mr Blair is pleased to be able to send you a contribution and hopes the enclosed copy of one of his favourite recipes will be suitable for inclusion in your book. It is sent with his best wishes.

Yours sincerely

MR S AUST

Prime Minister Mr Tony Blair is no exception and has kindly submitted this next recipe for Ragout of Lamb. I wonder which famous politicians and celebrities he has served this dish to?

74

Ragout of Lamb

Ingredients:

500g / 1lb stewing lamb
100g / 4oz onions
1 tin plum tomatoes
1 clove of garlic
Chopped coriander
1 green pepper
200g / 7oz button mushrooms
25g / 1oz flour
2 tablespoons olive oil
600ml / 1 pint brown stock

Method:

Fry seasoned meat in the oil with the onion, garlic and green pepper. Drain off excess oil and add flour. Cook out flour gently and then gradually add the stock and juice from the tomatoes.
Cook for 15 minutes before adding the chopped tomato and mushrooms.
Cook until meat is tender, check seasoning, and add coriander
Serve with coriander flavoured cous cous and garden vegetables.

Bill Clinton

Former President of the United States of America Bill Clinton responded to our rather tongue in cheek request for a recipe when we wrote to him at his New York office. We were delighted to receive his reply, for although he is no longer the leader of one of the most powerful nations in the world he is still a very busy man and we really appreciated the fact that he took time to support a charity that he had never heard of.

President Bill Clinton's Favorite Recipe: Chicken Enchiladas

Cooking oil	1 28-ounce can tomatoes	3 cups shredded, cooked chicken
2 4-ounce cans chopped green chilies	2 cups chopped onion	2 cups dairy sour cream
	2 teaspoons salt	2 cups grated cheddar cheese
1 large clove garlic, minced	1/2 teaspoon oregano	15 corn or flour tortillas

Preheat oil in skillet. Saute chopped chilies with minced garlic in oil. Drain and break up tomatoes; reserve 1/2 cup liquid. To chilies and garlic, add tomatoes, onion, 1 teaspoon salt, oregano and reserved tomato liquid. Simmer uncovered until thick, about 30 minutes. Remove from skillet and set aside. Combine chicken with sour cream, grated cheese and other teaspoon salt. Heat 1/3 cup oil; dip tortillas in oil until they become limp. Drain well on paper towels. Fill tortillas with chicken mixture; roll up and arrange side by side, seam down, in 9" x 13" x 2" baking dish. Pour tomato mixture over enchiladas and bake at 350 degrees until heated through, about 20 minutes. Yields 15 enchiladas.

President Bill Clinton's Favo(u)rite Recipe: Chicken Enchiladas

NB: AS THIS RECIPE IS IN AMERICAN CUP MEASURES, THE METRIC AND IMPERIAL MEASUREMENTS ARE APPROXIMATE

Ingredients:
Cooking oil
2x 110g / 4oz cans of chopped green chillies
1 large clove of garlic, minced
1 large can tomatoes
2 cups / 230g / 8oz chopped onions
2 tsp salt
½ tsp oregano
3 cups (425g /1lb approx) Shredded cooked chicken
2 cups / 150g / 5oz sour cream
2 cups / 115g / 3¼oz Grated Cheddar cheese
15 corn or flour tortillas

Method:
Pre heat the oil in a skillet (frying pan). Sauté chopped chillies with minced garlic in oil.
Drain and break up tomatoes; reserve ½ cup of liquid. To chillies and garlic, add tomatoes, onion, 1 tsp salt, oregano and reserved tomato liquid. Simmer uncovered until thick, about 30 minutes.
Remove from skillet and set aside. Combine chicken with sour cream, grated cheese and other tsp of salt. Heat ⅓ cup of oil; dip tortillas in oil until they become limp. Drain well on paper towel. Fill tortillas with chicken mixture; roll up and arrange side by side, seam side down, in 9"x 13" x 2" baking dish. Pour Tomato mixture over enchiladas and bake at 180°C until heated through, about 20 minutes. Yields 15 enchiladas.

Jenny Pitman O.B.E.

Jenny Pitman became one of the very first women to be granted a professional licence to train horses, she has trained winners of all five major Nationals and two Cheltenham Gold Cups. With Corbière in 1983, she became the first woman trainer to win the Grand National - and she is still the only one to have done so. Twelve years later, Royal Athlete won her this prestigious race for a second time.

Rib of Beef

7 Bone prime ribs of beef
2 to 3 tbsp peppercorns
1 tbsp course sea salt
3 to 4 tbsp fresh minced garlic
1 tsp dried rosemary
1tsp dried basil.

Method:

Pre heat oven to 230°C / 450°F / Gas Mark 8. Crush peppercorn, garlic, salt and herbs.
Place the beef fat side up, bone side down in a roasting tin rub with the mixture of garlic salt and herbs and cook for approx 25/30 minutes. Reduce the heat to 170°C / 325°F / Mark 3 and cook for a further 15 minutes per pound.
When the beef is done place on a large warm platter and stand for 10.15 minutes this will make it easier to carve. Serve with Roast Potatoes, Yorkshire Pudding and vegetables

Desserts

Sir Cliff Richard

Cliff Richard is often called the "Peter Pan of Pop". He was Britain's answer to Elvis in the late 50's and early 60's,'always hitting the right note' when choosing his latest record, which is why he is still having hit records after 40 years. Cliff now spends much of his time abroad, but his secretary forwarded this recipe for his favourite dessert.

Transkei Mud

Ingredients:
405g / 14oz can condensed milk
300ml / ½ pt double cream
200g / 7oz digestive biscuits
100g /3 ½ oz mint chocolate (such as Aero) grated

Method:

Boil the can of condensed milk unopened, and completely covered with water at all times, for about 2 hours. Allow it to cool fully, or overnight. Whisk the double cream until it stands in soft peaks. Slowly add the caramelised milk, one spoonful at a time. Mix thoroughly. Grate all the chocolate, then, reserving a little for decoration, add it to the mixture and stir in. Layer the mixture into a glass serving dish, alternating with the digestive biscuits, making three layers of each. Refrigerate overnight. Sprinkle over the remaining chocolate before serving. (If feeling particularly indulgent, whip a second lot of double cream until stiff, and spread this over the pudding before decorating with remaining chocolate). Serve in small portions, as this pudding is very rich.

Preparation time: 20 Minutes
Cooking Time: 2 Hours (plus overnight cooling for condensed milk, and overnight refrigeration for pudding)

Julie Carr

Julie wrote: 'I have worked for Duchess of Kent House as a uni Secretary for 7 years.
This recipe was found in a 'Round the World' cookbook originally and has been slightly modified.
I am a terrible cook according to my husband, with many culinary disasters to my name, but if I can make this and it tastes delicious, then I am positive it must be foolproof.'

Crème Brulée Ice Cream (Serves 6)

Ingredients:
525ml / 18 fl oz creamy milk
3 strips lemon zest
115g / 4 oz caster sugar
1 cinnamon stick
4 egg yolks
1 tbsp corn flour
55g / 2oz Demerara sugar
2 tbsp water

Method:
Bring the milk to a simmer with the lemon zest/ cinnamon stick/ castor sugar, stirring gently. Turn off the heat and leave to infuse for 20 minutes. Beat the egg yolks and corn flour with a wooden spoon in a bowl which fits over a pan of simmering water. Strain the hot milk into the egg mixture. Stir over the simmering water until the custard coats the back of the spoon. Pour into small bread tin and then freeze for two hours. Put Demerara sugar and water into a small saucepan. Heat until it smells of caramel then without hesitating pour onto a sheet of foil laid out on a board. Wait until it has set and when hard snap it up and grind in a blender or processor. Remove custard ice-cream from freezer and beat well with a fork. Stir 3 tbsp caramel into the ice-cream and freeze until firm. Soften in fridge for 30 minutes and sprinkle with remaining caramel before serving.

John Madejski

Reading's John Madejski has come a long way from his days working for one of the town's newspapers, he went on to found his own company Auto Trader and is the man behind Reading Football Club, he was responsible for the wonderful new football ground the Madejski Stadium. John said in his letter that he didn't cook but nevertheless sent this next recipe for inclusion in the book.

Athol Brose Dessert
(Serves 6)

Ingredients:

50g / 2oz medium oatmeal
600ml / 1pt double cream
75g / 3oz honey
50ml / 2fl oz whisky

Method:

Toast the oatmeal in a dry pan over a medium heat until it colours very slightly and smells warm. Allow to cool. Whisk the cream, honey and whisky until it forms soft, gentle drifts. Do this gently, by hand, taking great care not to over whisk. Fold in the cold oatmeal. Spoon the mixture into six small glasses and place in the fridge for an hour or so before serving.

Terry Wogan OBE

One of my most embarrassing moments:

'I well remember Monday 18th February 1985. It was the first evening of the new thrice weekly 'WOGAN 'which came live from the BBC Television Theatre in Shepherds Bush.
One of my guests was Sir Elton John. I left my chair to walk over to greet Elton who was standing by the piano, went to shake hands and tripped, not very elegantly, and ended up on the floor with Elton trying to bring me to my feet. After several jolly japes from Elton I regained my composure (I think) and we carried on with the show. Not a very auspicious start to a new series, but it certainly made the papers the next day and, much to my mortification guests still came onto WOGAN to remind me of that first evening which always brought a flush to the old cheeks.'

Rich Chocolate Ice Cream

Terry's family love anything with chocolate in it. Here is a delicious recipe for one of their favourite ways of enjoying a chocolate dessert ...

Ingredients:

6 egg yolks
125g / 4oz caster sugar
900 ml / 1½ pints of double cream
5 ml / 1 tsp of vanilla essence
325g / 12oz plain chocolate

Method:

Whisk the egg yolks and caster sugar together until the mixture is very light and pale. Break the plain chocolate into the mixture and heat gently over a pan of simmering water, stirring all the time, until the mixture coats the back of a wooden spoon and the chocolate is completely melted. It is important that you <u>do not</u> allow the mixture to boil. Once this is done, then let it cool. Pour the cool chocolate mixture into a freezer proof container and freeze for about 5 hours (Terry adds 2 tbsp of Grand Marnier to the mixture before freezing it helps to keep it moist). Put in the fridge for about 20 minutes before serving with some nice fruit like strawberries with a raspberry coulis.

Joanna Lumley

From the Absolutely Fabulous Joanna Lumley.

A dessert that Patsy and Eddy would love to indulge themselves with - washed down with a bottle or two of bubbly!

Paradise Pudding

Ingredients:

300 ml / ½ Pint double cream
300 ml / ½ Pint Greek yoghurt
Dark brown sugar

Method:

Mix together gently with a spoon, put into a shallow dish and sprinkle with dark brown sugar. After 2 hours in the fridge, it will have turned into Paradise Pudding.

Jenny & Jim Mason

For many years Jenny and Jim Mason had a stall in Reading Market, then a few years ago they decided to come in from the cold and set up shop in Tilehurst. They are a lovely, friendly couple who always have a welcoming smile and always find time for a chat. Jenny admits that she is not a fan of cooking, but she and Jim got together and sent this next recipe.

Stuffed Pears in Apricot Sauce

Ingredients:

½ litre/ 1 pint dry white wine
125g / 4 oz sugar
150g / 5oz fresh apricots or 60g / 2oz of dried apricots (no need to soak)
125g / 4 oz low fat Ricotta cheese
15g / ½ oz plain chocolate
½ lemon
4 large ripe, but firm pears
4 chocolate leaves (optional)

Method:

Combine the wine with 100g / 3½ oz of the sugar and ½ litre of water in a large saucepan over a medium heat. Bring the liquid to a simmer; meanwhile peel the pears leaving the stems attached. As you work, lightly rub the ½ lemon over the pears to keep them from discolouring. Using a melon baller or a small spoon, core the pears from the bottom.
Squeeze the lemon ½ into the saucepan and then add the lemon shell to the liquid.
Carefully lower the pears into the simmering liquid, poach the pears for about 10 minutes turning ½ way through. While the pears are cooking you can prepare the apricots, if you are using fresh apricots blanch them in boiling water for 30 seconds to loosen the skins. Then peel and stone them, whether you use dried or fresh apricots chop them coarsely.
Remove the pears from the liquid with a slotted spoon and leave them upright on a plate to drain. Refrigerate the pears and reserve ½ Litre / 16 oz of the liquid, discard the rest. Add all but 2 tbsp of the apricot to the poaching liquid until it is reduced to approximately 6 fl oz, (takes about 15 minutes). Now puree the apricots and the liquid in a food processor or your blender. Refrigerate the purée.
While poaching liquid is reducing you can mix together, the chocolate, the remaining sugar and the reserved 2 tbsp of apricots. To serve fill each pear with Ricotta mixture, pour some of the apricot puree on to each plate and set the stuffed pear in the centre and garnish it with a chocolate leaf if you wish.

Or you could for a special occasion coat the whole pear with melted chocolate. Worry about the calories another day!!!

Cakes, Biscuits & Preserves

Shirley Ford

Shirley is a determined member of the Fundraising Committee and has raised money for us at Grovelands Medical Centre as well as helping at events.

Shirl's Coffee Time Favourite

Ingredients:
225g / 8oz self raising flour
225g / 8oz soft margarine
225g / 8oz caster sugar
4 medium eggs
2 tsp coffee with a little water mixed to a runny consistency

Method:
Sieve flour, cream, margarine with sugar, beat eggs and stir in carefully a little at a time.
Add a little flour and stir in gently. Continue in this way until thoroughly mixed. Lightly grease 2 sandwich tins (20cm) and divide the mixture equally. Bake for 20 minutes at 180°C / 350°F / Gas Mark 5
Turn out on to wire rack to cool.
For the Icing:
75g / 3oz Icing Sugar
50g / 2oz Butter
1 tsp coffee mixed with a little water.
Method:
Cream butter, add sifted icing sugar. Add coffee mixture a little at a time. When the cake is cool spread between two layers and spread the top with any remaining icing.

Suzanne Goodin

Suzanne was the driving force behind our first fundraising book, Deliciously Famous. She wrote then:
'This next cake is called the disappearing cake, because that's what happened to it the day I took it in to work for a friend to decorate as a ruby wedding present. I must explain. We at Grovelands Medical Centre love food and someone is always bringing in cakes - they get left in the kitchen and we all help ourselves. This particular Monday morning I was running a bit late, so I dumped the cake on the side and rushed to open up the appointments line. Hazel our housekeeper came in later to make us all coffee saw the cake and, yes you've guessed…….. still everyone enjoyed it! Poor Hazel felt terrible about it. I just thought it was hilarious. Someone went out to buy a replacement and I think Jacquie decorated that. It's never been forgotten, least of all by Hazel.'

Rich Fruit Cake

Ingredients:
225g / 8oz butter
225g / 8oz brown sugar
225g / 8oz plain flour
225g / 8oz sultanas
225g / 8oz raisins
225g / 8oz currants
4 medium eggs
Pinch of salt
½ tsp spice
½ tsp nutmeg
75g / 3oz glacé cherries
1 tbsp black treacle

Method:
Cream butter and sugar, add lightly beaten eggs. Fold in salt, spices and flour. Add fruit and treacle and mix well. Bake in a slow oven at 150°C / 290°F / Gas mark 2, for approximately 3 ½ - 4 hours. Allow cake to cool before removing from tin and pour brandy on cold cake.

Delia Smith

Delia Smith needs no introduction. She says this is her favourite cake,... 'it's simple but absolute heaven. The spiciness of the ginger within the moist cake, coupled with the sharpness of the lemon icing is such that it never fails to please all who eat it.'

Preserved Ginger Cake with Lemon Icing

Ingredients: (makes 15 squares)

5 pieces preserved stem ginger in syrup, chopped
2 tbsp ginger syrup (from jar of stem ginger in syrup)
1 heaped tsp ground ginger
1 heaped tsp grated fresh ginger
175g butter at room temperature, plus a little extra for greasing
175g golden caster sugar
3 large eggs at room temperature
1 tbsp molasses syrup
225g self raising flour
1 tbsp ground almonds
2 tbsp milk

For the topping:
Juice 1 lemon
225g unrefined golden icing sugar
2 extra pieces preserved stem ginger in syrup

You will also need:
Non-stick cake tin 15 x 25 cm, 2.5 cm deep and some silicone paper(parchment)measuring 25 x 35 cm
Pre-heat oven to 170 °C

Method:
First prepare the cake tin by greasing it lightly and lining it with the silicone paper: press it into the tin, folding the corners in to make it fit neatly(see Book One) – the paper should come up 2.5cm above the edge.

To make the cake, take a large mixing bowl and cream the butter and sugar together until light and fluffy. Next break the eggs into a jug and beat them with a fork until fluffy, then gradually beat them into the mixture, a little at a time, until all the egg is incorporated. Next fold in the ginger syrup and molasses; the best way to add the molasses is to lightly grease a tablespoon, then take a tablespoon of molasses and just push it off the spoon with a rubber spatula into the mixture. Now sift the flour and ground ginger onto a plate, then gradually fold these in, about a tablespoon at a time. Next fold in the almonds, followed by the milk, and lastly the grated ginger root and pieces of stem ginger. Now spread the cake mixture evenly in the cake tin, then bake on the middle shelf of the oven for 45-50 minutes, or until the cake has risen, springy and firm to the touch in the centre. Leave the cake to cool in the tin for 10 minutes, then turn it out onto a wire rack and make sure it is absolutely cold before you attempt to ice it.

For the icing, sift the icing sugar into a bowl and mix with enough of the lemon juice to make the consistency of thick cream – you might not need all the lemon juice. Now spread the icing all over the top of the cake, and don't worry if it dribbles down the sides in places, as this looks quite attractive. Cut the remaining ginger into 15 chunks, and place these in lines across the cake so that when you cut it you will have 15 squares, each with a piece of ginger in the centre. It's absolute heaven. If you'd like one or two of these cakes tucked away for a rainy day, they freeze beautifully – simply defrost and put the icing on half an hour before serving.

Copyright Delia Smith 1999 – Recipe reproduced by permission from Delia's How to Cook Book Two (Published by BBC Worldwide)

Sir Matthew Pinsent

Matthew is a Triple Olympic Gold Medallist and of course team mate of Sir Steve Redgrave. Matthew is a member of the Leander Club in Henley-on-Thames and has sent this recipe for flapjacks.

The recipe is given in cups. I have had trouble in finding out the equivalent metric / imperial weights. I was told by the Good Housekeeping Magazine that the cup measurements were available from cookware departments in most stores.

Dee's Awesome Flapjacks

Ingredients:

½ cup butter
½ cup sugar
1/3 cup apricot jam
2¼ cups of oats.

Method:

Mix all the ingredients together. Squash in a tin lined with baking parchment and cook for 8 - 10 minutes at 190°C / 375°F / Gas Mark 4.

Paul Farmer

Paul is another volunteer at the Duchess of Kent House and helps out in the fundraising office on Tuesdays. He is also a keen helper at our events, especially the Hospice Awareness Month in June each year where the theme colour is yellow and he obliges by dyeing his hair and beard yellow!

Celebration Cake

Ingredients:

2 lb / 900g mixed fruit
300 ml / ½ pint of water
3 tbsp vegetable oil
1 tbsp dark treacle
1 tsp mixed spice
Grated rind of 1 lemon
Grated rind of 1 orange
395g / 14 oz self-raising wholemeal flour

Method:

Mix the fruit, the water, oil, spices and grated orange and lemon rind together.
Sift in the flour and mix well, grease and line a large cake tin, spoon in the mixture and bake in the centre of the oven for approx 3 hours at 110 °C / 225 °F / Gas mark 1.
After 1 hour cover with greaseproof paper to prevent from burning.

This cake is suitable for vegan and diabetic diets.

Gill Johnson

Gill's jams, marmalades and preserves are fabulous and go in a flash. Personal favourite is the blackberry and apple, which she makes at the end of August when the fruit is ripe.
Gill is a Queen's Guide and has been involved locally in Reading, with the Girl Guides Organisation for over 10 years.

Blackberry and Apple Jam

Pare, core and thinly slice some good cooking apples (as sharp a kind as possible, but ripe) and put ¼ lb of the slices to each pound / ½ kg of ripe and dry berries.

800g / 1¾ lb jam sugar is required to every 900g / 2 lb of mixed fruit.

Put the fruit and sugar into a preserving pan and stir well with a wooden spoon, until the juice runs from the berries, then bring just to the boil and simmer for 30 minutes.

Test by putting a little on a saucer and put this into the freezer for 2 minutes, and if it jellies (wrinkles when touched after tipping slightly) it is done.

Remove the pan from the heat and let it stand a few minutes before potting. Pour the hot jam into the dry, warm pots and screw on the jar tops, label the jars with the name, date and allow to cool.
Delicious on toast, or with ice cream!

Nadia Black

Nadia is a freelance secretary and has worked on several occasions in Duchess of Kent House. Now a permanent member of staff, Nadia writes: 'I got the chocolate chip cookie recipe from my mother-in-law having been given it by a college friend of her daughters. The recipe had originally come from a restaurant in America. A lady had liked the cookies so much; she asked the restaurant if she could buy a copy of the recipe. They said she would have to pay two fifty for it and she agreed and it was charged to her credit card. When she received the bill, she found she had been charged $250. She contacted the restaurant and they said that was correct. The woman was under the impression she was going to pay $2.50. Anyway, there was nothing she could do but pay the $250.00. She was so annoyed that she photocopied the recipe and gave it out free to everyone she knew and has asked people to pass it on to as many of their friends / colleagues as possible. So, that is the story behind the recipe.'

Chocolate Chip Cookies (makes 28 Cookies)

Ingredients:
½ cup of butter or margarine
1 cup plain flour
½ tsp baking soda
½ cup sugar
1¼ cup oatmeal (blended)
6 oz chocolate chips
½ cup brown sugar
Method:
Blend the oatmeal to a fine powder, cream both sugars and butter together, and add the egg and vanilla essence and mix. In a separate bowl mix together flour, oatmeal, salt, baking powder and baking soda. Mix the contents of the two bowls together. Add the chocolate chips, grated chocolate and nuts. Roll into balls and place 5 cm / 2" apart on a cookie sheet. Bake for 10 minutes at 375°F / 190°C / Gas Mark 5.

Donations

We hope that you have enjoyed this book.
Duchess of Kent House Trust welcomes your donation to continue our funding of this Specialist Palliative Care unit serving in-patient, out-patient and day therapy patients.

Cheques should be made payable to:
Duchess of Kent House Trust
and sent to
Duchess of Kent House Trust
22 Liebenrood Rd
Reading
RG30 2DX

Donations may be made online at our website:
www.duchessofkenthouse.org,uk
Should you wish to remember us in your Will please quote our charity registration number, which is 1085912.

giftaid it

Most personal donations are eligible for tax relief under the Gift Aid tax scheme – please ask for further details.

Thank you so much for your support.